THE GIFT
of PRAYER

CHARLES F. STANLEY

THOMAS NELSON
Since 1798

Published in Nashville, Tennessee, by Thomas Nelson. Thomas Nelson is a registered trademark of HarperCollins Christian Publishing, Inc.

Thomas Nelson titles may be purchased in bulk for educational, business, fund-raising, or sales promotional use. For information, please email SpecialMarkets@ThomasNelson.com.

Unless otherwise noted, Scripture quotations are taken from the New American Standard Bible®, Copyright © 1960, 1962, 1963, 1968, 1971, 1972, 1973, 1975, 1977, 1995 by The Lockman Foundation. Used by permission. (www.Lockman.org)

Scripture quotations marked KJV are taken from the King James Version. Public domain.

Scripture quotations marked NLT are taken from the Holy Bible, New Living Translation. © 1996, 2004, 2007, 2013, 2015 by Tyndale House Foundation. Used by permission of Tyndale House Publishers, Inc., Carol Stream, Illinois 60188. All rights reserved.

Scripture quotations marked TLB are taken from The Living Bible. Copyright © 1971. Used by permission of Tyndale House Publishers, Inc., Carol Stream, Illinois 60188. All rights reserved.

Any Internet addresses, phone numbers, or company or product information printed in this book are offered as a resource and are not intended in any way to be or to imply an endorsement by Thomas Nelson, nor does Thomas Nelson vouch for the existence, content, or services of these sites, phone numbers, companies, or products beyond the life of this book.

ISBN-13: 978-1-4002-1577-5

Printed in China

19 20 21 22 23 WAI 10 9 8 7 6 5 4 3 2 1

CONTENTS

1

AN OPEN INVITATION

What is it worth to you to have someone you can always go to for help and counsel?

Who is always willing to comfort and strengthen you?

Who unfailingly has answers to your questions?

Who never falters in guiding you perfectly in your choices and giving you wisdom for your path?

Who has the power to heal any wound you may have, break through any barrier you may encounter, overcome any obstacle you may face, and attain victory over any challenge that assails you?

And who would never leave, reject, or abandon you?

It would be worth a lot to have someone like that in your corner, wouldn't it?

The good news is that if you are a believer in Jesus Christ, you have just that. You are the beneficiary of the great honor of having an open and permanent invitation into the presence of the Great I Am. Hebrews 4:16 describes that amazing privilege with these wonderful words: "Let us draw near with confidence to the throne of grace, so that we may receive mercy and find grace to help in time of need."

In other words, *you have that Someone.*

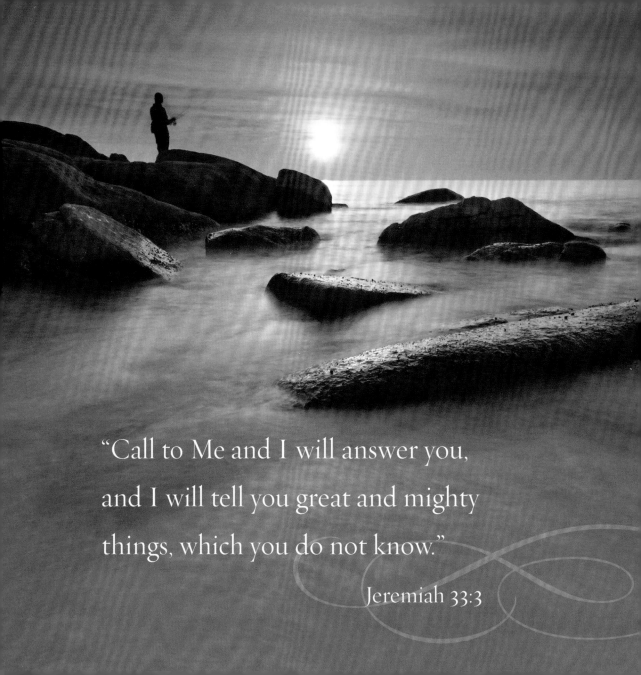

"Call to Me and I will answer you, and I will tell you great and mighty things, which you do not know."

Jeremiah 33:3

That is the awe-inspiring honor you have through the gift of prayer.

You have been beckoned to engage in an intimate dialogue with the One who not only holds the whole universe in His hand but who cares about you most and best knows your inner workings and potential. You have the unique opportunity to ask the Lord of all that exists to guide you in the steps you take, deliver you in the areas where you cannot help yourself, and answer all that confounds you. Even better, you get to know *Him*.

Naturally, you may have doubts about this—not only that a conversation with the God of the universe is possible but that you have an open invitation as His child. Perhaps you would say that you pray but are not really sure He hears or will answer you. You hope so, of course, but may not have total confidence that He will respond or that you are worthy of His attention. Is the Creator of heaven and earth really *that* available to you? That willing to hear and help you?

Friend, God never intended for you to approach Him with a "hope so" attitude. He wants you to know *for certain* that your good, loving, and powerful heavenly Father is always available to listen to your cries and respond to your prayers. As He promises in Jeremiah

33:3, "Call to Me and I will answer you, and I will tell you great and mighty things, which you do not know."

Your loving God desires to communicate with you. I can say this for certain because I've experienced a deeply personal relationship with Him through prayer. I am constantly amazed at the insights and principles the Father shows me in His Word during periods of quiet, prayerful meditation. When I've had to face painful trials, His loving comfort and guidance have helped me emerge triumphant and stronger in spirit rather than defeated and weaker. And I can only attribute anything productive or effective in my ministry to His wisdom and power.

He has been a constant Helper, a faithful Friend, a victorious Defender, a wise Leader, and a great Redeemer to me, and He can be all of that to you too. You can experience God as deeply and intimately as I have.

Is that what you desire: deep insight and understanding? Comfort and guidance that help you triumph in your trials? Wisdom and power that lead you to success in life? These are the rewards of vibrant, steadfast, continuing fellowship with God. The best part is that you

You have been beckoned to engage
in an intimate dialogue with the One
who not only holds the whole universe
in His hand but who cares about you.

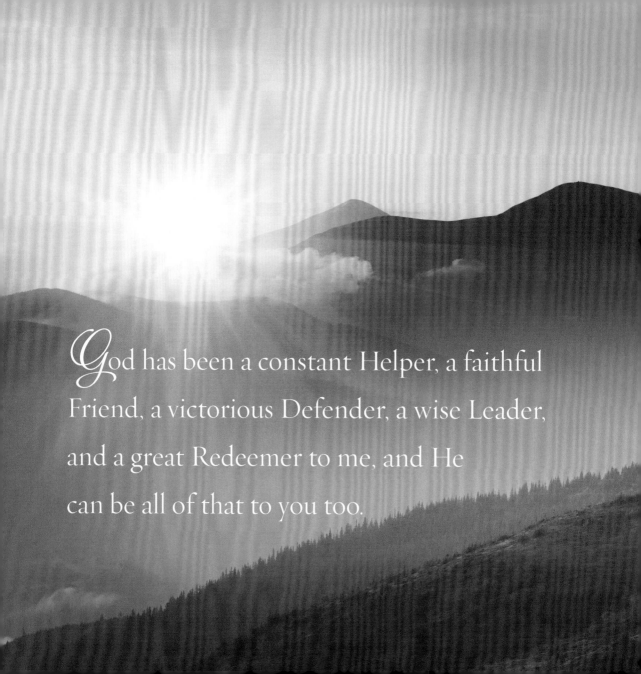

God has been a constant Helper, a faithful Friend, a victorious Defender, a wise Leader, and a great Redeemer to me, and He can be all of that to you too.

don't need anything extra to enjoy His love and wisdom—just an open heart that hungers to really know Him.

The Lord longs for you to receive and use this gift of prayer every day of your life. In fact, your God wanted it so much, He paid the price so you could have it.

You see, though this honor to approach His throne is free to us, it was very costly to Him. We are all separated from Him because of our sinfulness (Romans 3:23)—those very mistakes, flaws, weaknesses, and sins that make us feel unworthy of His presence. But that is why Jesus came to forgive our sins (2 Corinthians 5:17–21). Through His death on the cross and His resurrection, Jesus paid the penalty of our sin and restored our ability to have an eternal, everlasting relationship with the Father. He gave us the ability to pray and have the deepest cries of our hearts heard by the God who can help us.

What does salvation through Jesus accomplish for us? It means that you and I never have to feel unworthy when approaching the Lord. We never have to feel shame in God's presence when we know Jesus as our Savior. We are absolutely forgiven, completely cleansed of all we've ever done wrong.

As I said, our privilege of an ongoing conversation with God was very costly to Him, but because of the completeness of His payment, it is an absolutely awesome gift that you can never lose. And because of what Jesus has done, your invitation into God's presence is always open. Always.

You may be thinking, *I've never trusted Jesus as my Savior. I've never entered into a relationship with God. But I would like to.*

It is not difficult; Jesus has done all the work for you. All you need to do is accept His provision by faith (Ephesians 2:8–9). Acknowledge that you have sinned and ask Him to forgive you. You can tell Him in your own words or use this simple prayer:

Lord Jesus, I ask You to forgive my sins and save me from eternal separation from God. By faith, I accept Your death on the cross and resurrection as sufficient payment for all I have ever done wrong. Thank You for providing the way for me to know and to have a relationship with You. Through faith in You, I have eternal life and can enjoy intimate fellowship with God. Thank You for giving me an open invitation to enjoy Your presence. Teach me to pray—to seek You and know You. And help me to always follow Your leadership. In Jesus' name, amen.

I can still remember the Sunday I prayed a prayer—my first real prayer—like this to Jesus and came to know Him as my personal Savior. I was twelve, and I recall sitting in church with my buddies, Nelson, Clyde, Tig, and James.

I did not know the Father at all at that point. I knew *about* Him, but I did not yet understand how He could be with me every moment of every day—present and available for everything I faced.

All the nights that my mother and I knelt by my bed, I had relied on my mother's prayers to be answered, not mine. But as I repented of my sin and asked Jesus into my heart that day at church, that all changed. From that day on, I began to *know* Him and enjoy the gift He had given me—the gift of Himself.

Perhaps this is what you would like as well:

- to experience and understand the awesome, real, unending privilege of God's presence, wisdom, comfort, guidance, protection, provision, and understanding
- to know God, grow in your relationship with Him, and find greater fulfillment in your life
- to hear His voice and to enjoy an active, meaningful, ongoing

Because of what Jesus has done, your invitation into God's presence is always open. Always.

conversation with the Lord of all creation that will continue into eternity

If so, then rejoice. Because you have an open invitation. The great gift of prayer awaits you so you can know the loving, all-knowing, all-powerful Giver of the gift, who is with you forever no matter what you face.

Let's not wait. Let us pray!

Father, how grateful we are that You desire to communicate with us and give us an open invitation to Your presence. That You have reconciled us to Yourself through the death and resurrection of Your Son, Jesus Christ. That You have given us the awesome privilege of prayer to strengthen and deepen our relationships with You. Father, we answer, "Yes!" Usher us into Your presence and teach us about this great gift of prayer. But even more, Father, draw us into an intimate relationship with You, teaching us how to connect with You in deeper, more meaningful ways than ever before and trust You for every step we take. In Jesus' matchless name, we pray. Amen.

THE GRACIOUSNESS
of the GIVER

$\mathcal{P}$rayer is an intimate conversation with the God of all that exists, and your relationship with Him determines the impact of your life and the influence you have with those around you.

2

THE PATHWAY
TO FULFILLMENT

*R*elationally, your greatest needs as a person are to know that you are loved, respected, valued, accepted, capable, and secure. It's important that you know for certain that someone cares for you as you are—but who also can help you become all you were created to be. This need will motivate you in untold ways.

Perhaps you strive to achieve great things so you can feel worthwhile to others. Or maybe you struggle to prove that you are worthy of people's admiration in other ways—by being the smartest, toughest, funniest, most attractive, or wealthiest person in the room. It's even possible that you hide parts of yourself from others in order to diminish the pain of loneliness and isolation you feel, but you've only succeeded in increasing it.

Whether you admit it or not, you're endeavoring to fill your most profound internal needs in ways that actually don't work—not really.

Prayer is the ultimate pathway to meeting these needs because it is the way you can know the One who truly fulfills them. I have often said, "Our intimacy with God, His highest priority for our lives, determines the impact of our lives." Why is intimacy so important?

Because it is only through such a close relationship with Jesus that your deepest and most important longings are truly met.

Prayer ushers you into a relationship with your Creator that impacts and reveals who you are as a person at the most profound levels—in places you may not even know exist. It is the kind of inter-action that reaches into your most private thoughts and issues of identity and exposes the most difficult places in a manner that is redemptive and healing.

Likewise, when you get that close to Jesus through prayer, you learn to see yourself through His eyes. You realize that you were created for more than what you're living, and you gain the courage to go after it. In other words, a truly intimate relationship with Christ through prayer is healing, revealing, and motivating—bringing out the very best in you.

Friend, the Lord God created you, knows everything about you, and always does what is best for you—every time and in all situations. And whether you realize it or not, there is a longing within you to know God and be known by Him. This happens to a depth within you that is untouched by human comprehension or earthly substitu-tions. But you have the awesome privilege of accessing it through the gift of prayer.

"I have loved you with an everlasting love; therefore I have drawn you with lovingkindness."

Jeremiah 31:3

$\mathcal{P}$rayer ushers you into a relationship with your Creator that impacts and reveals who you are as a person at the most profound levels.

Additionally, not only is your intimacy with God important for you personally, but you can reach the full potential of your life only as you walk with Him in consistent, continuing communion. Your life was made to be an earthen vessel that shines forth His glory (2 Corinthians 4:7). And the more you know Christ and are unified with Him, the more He lives His life through you, giving you His power and revealing His plan for you.

That is why it is only through a prayer-based intimacy with God that your needs are truly fulfilled. From Him flows all that is lacking in you and all that is possible through you.

Of course, communicating with God is one thing, but truly knowing Him is another. You may wonder: *How can I know for sure that I am capable of that kind of relationship with Jesus or that He really sees me as worthy of it?* To answer this, I invite you to consider how the Lord created you. He formed you in His image and likeness—with intellect, emotions, and a will that provide a platform from which you can relate to Him. What other creature exhibits such a capacity or has been given such an honor? He fashioned you in such a manner for one reason—so you could know Him in the deepest parts of your being, personally and intimately.

Likewise, remember that before salvation, you were spiritually dead. You did not and could not seek the Lord on your own. Romans 3:11 affirms, "There is none who understands, there is none who seeks for God." Without the ability to interact with the Father *spiritually*, you cannot truly know Him. This is why Jesus said, "No one can come to Me unless the Father who sent Me draws him" (John 6:44).

In every instance throughout Scripture, God is the One who takes the initiative in the relationship between Himself and humanity, because only He has the power and ability to bridge the spiritual gap that is between us. And He takes the responsibility to make you capable of communicating with Him. In fact, this is the very reason Christ made such a costly sacrifice to save you and give you a new nature—so that you would be able to interact with Him and know Him on the most profoundly intimate level, which is through prayer.

But why? Why has God gone through all this trouble to relate to you intimately and to give you the gift of prayer? I believe we can find the answer to this in Revelation 4:11 (KJV): "Thou hast created all things, and for thy pleasure they are and were created." In other words, God created you because it gave Him joy to do so. He delights in actively expressing His love and revealing Himself to you. And He gave you the gift of prayer so you could receive His love for you, and you could respond to Him in turn.

When you feel those deep desires to be loved, respected, valued, accepted, capable, and secure, understand that God is drawing you to Himself (Jeremiah 31:3). He is, without a doubt, calling you to profound fellowship with Him in order to bring out the very best in you and empower you to be all He created you to be. He is inviting you to a deep, intimate relationship with Him. He is beckoning you to prayer.

Therefore, say yes to Him! Entrust yourself to the One who loves you most and has given so much for you to know Him.

Lord Jesus, thank You for the gift of prayer in which I can have intimate fellowship with You and find the profound, satisfying fulfillment I long for. I open my heart to You, Jesus. Heal what is wounded, reveal what is contrary to Your best, and empower me to live the life You desire for me. Even now, I accept that what Your Holy Spirit brings to mind is what You desire to deal with in my life. I confess my sins to You, Lord Jesus, because You are faithful and just to forgive my sins and cleanse me from all unrighteousness (1 John 1:9). I know that You are setting me free and healing the painful places of my life. I also realize that You are preparing me for greater purposes than I can imagine. Thank You, Lord Jesus! Thank You for drawing me close, giving me the gift of prayer, communing with me, and showing me Your path of life. In all things I trust You and look to You for love, wisdom, strength, and guidance. In Jesus' name, amen.

The more you know Christ and are unified with Him, the more He lives His life through you, giving you His power and revealing His plan for you.

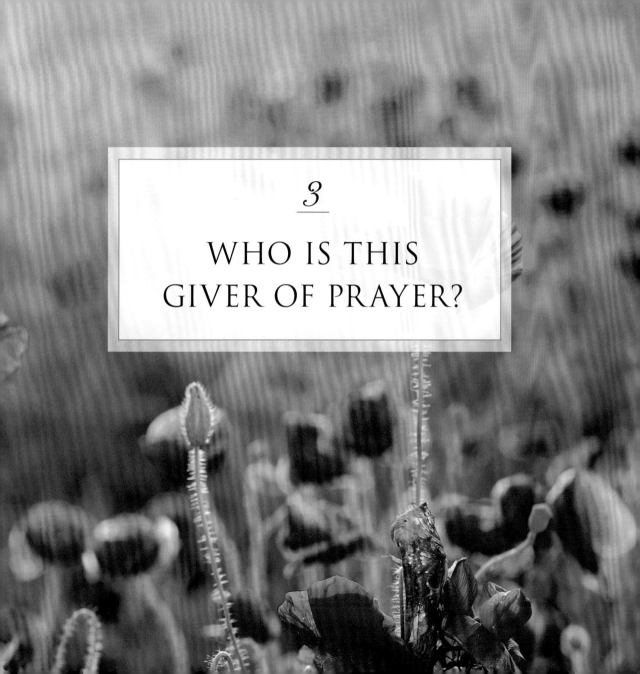

3

WHO IS THIS
GIVER OF PRAYER?

*T*he first privilege of having an intimate relationship with God through prayer is that you get to know God. Consider what a great and awesome honor that is—to know the One who not only created all that exists but also directs it from His mighty throne.

This is an amazing thought when you consider how often we long for favor from those in authority over us or to have help from someone powerful enough to change our circumstances. We see it every day in the way people clamor for the attention of the powerful, famous, skilled, and wealthy. It can seem that we are subject to other people's biases, evil desires, mistakes, and faulty reasoning. We may even fall into the false belief that our futures are *dependent* on their help and their decisions.

So even though we may acknowledge that God exists, it's possible that we feel responsible to resolve difficulties on our own or seek earthly assistance rather than taking our troubles to Him. From our narrow, earthbound points of view, perhaps we see no hope in our situations, no solutions to our dilemmas, and no end to our sufferings. When we go before Him, we may do so with our own limitations and the hope of help from other people in mind.

But Proverbs 29:26 reminds us, "Many seek the ruler's favor, but justice for man comes from the LORD." Your deliverance—regardless of the vessel used to achieve it—always comes from God Himself. In fact, nothing can touch your life without first being allowed by the hand of your Creator, who formed you in your mother's womb and ensures that what you experience will work for greater purposes when you follow Him (Romans 8:28).

That's what makes the gift of prayer so powerful and impactful—*the One to whom we pray.* We are interacting with the Almighty, our Lord, Maker, King, Mighty Warrior, Redeemer, and faithful High Priest. He is the true source of our help!

The Father proclaims, "Behold, I am the LORD, the God of all flesh; is anything too difficult for Me?" (Jeremiah 32:27). No, there is absolutely *nothing* too challenging for Him to overcome!

But perhaps you are wondering, *Why should I pray to God to know Him? Will it really make a difference? Does He really care about me? Can I really trust Him?*

It is normal to have these kinds of questions, especially if the people in your life have disappointed you, have been dishonest, or have acted in a manner contrary to your best interest. But you can

Consider what a great and awesome honor that is—to know the One who not only created all that exists but who also directs it from His mighty throne.

be certain that the Father will unfailingly do what is good, loving, and righteous on your behalf because He loves you and always does the right thing (Numbers 23:19; Psalm 22:3–4). And as you interact with Him in prayer, you understand this in increasingly profound and wonderful ways.

This is why the writer of Hebrews proclaimed, "It is impossible for God to lie. Therefore, we who have fled to him for refuge can have great confidence as we hold to the hope that lies before us" (6:18 NLT). When the Father says He cares for you, it is not a trick; it is the truth. He will never lead you astray but will always be honorable and guide you in the best way possible. So yes, you can trust the Lord's wonderful character. And the more you know Him, the more you will trust Him.

Of course, the next questions you may have are, *Can God help me? Is He able to make something of my situation?* After all, the value of any promise is based not only on the character of the person making the guarantee but also on the *capacity* to fulfill it.

Let me assure you, God has *never* failed to keep His word. Solomon proclaimed in 1 Kings 8:56, "Blessed be the LORD . . . not one word has failed of all His good promise." He is absolutely capable

THE GIFT of PRAYER

of fulfilling your needs—sufficiently wise, strong, and loving to help you, no matter how overwhelming your circumstances may seem.

This is because God is *sovereign*; He is the majestic Ruler of all creation. He set the laws of nature in place. Matter, space, and time are in His hand and under His authority. Psalm 103:19 tells us, "The LORD has established His throne in the heavens, and His sovereignty rules over all."

What does this mean for your situation? First, the Father is *omnipotent*—He is all-powerful. He can literally move heaven and earth to accomplish His will for you because He put them in place and guides their every movement (Psalm 104). As you fellowship with Him in prayer, He not only fills you with His strength but supernaturally clears away obstacles for you.

Also, the Lord is *omniscient*, which signifies He is all-knowing and completely wise. He sees your past, present, and future and understands everything about your situation, even details you could not possibly discern. He identifies exactly what you need and how to provide it, but He also uses your difficulties to build you up and mature your faith (Romans 8:28). As you engage in the gift of prayer, not only does God give you His supernatural insight and wisdom, but

If God is for us, who is against us? He who did not spare His own Son, but delivered Him over for us all, how will He not also with Him freely give us all things?

Romans 8:31–32

you experience the astounding manner in which He teaches you and navigates your path in brilliant ways you could never have figured out on your own.

Additionally, God is *omnipresent.* He is outside of time, and everything that exists is in His presence, so He is always with you in every moment, no matter where you go (Joshua 1:9). Nothing in your life escapes His notice. He is able to rally resources and influence circumstances that you don't even know exist in order to solve the problems you're facing, regardless of what they are. So as you come before His throne of grace, you not only have the assurance of His awesome presence, but you become aware that "neither death, nor life, nor angels, nor principalities, nor things present, nor things to come, nor powers, nor height, nor depth, nor any other created thing, will be able to separate us from the love of God, which is in Christ Jesus our Lord" (Romans 8:38–39). Even if something is completely out of your control, it is still in His, and therefore you are safe in His care.

Luke 1:37 affirms, "Nothing will be impossible with God." No matter how complicated, confusing, untenable, or overwhelming the trials you face, the living Lord is greater and can lead you to victory in them (John 16:33). So again, the response is *yes*, the Father really is *able* to help you.

Of course, the final question on your heart may be the most personal and even the most painful one: *Does God really want to help me?*

This is the question many of us struggle to answer. Although we may accept that God is trustworthy and capable of delivering us from our troubles, we are not certain that He is *willing* to do so. These doubts often stem from feelings of inadequacy. We doubt we are worthy of His love and presence.

First, understand that the Lord accepts us based on Christ's death on the cross, not because of what we have done or have failed to do (Ephesians 2:8–9). As I said in the previous chapters, you and I can have a relationship with the Father only through the salvation Jesus provides.

However, once we trust Christ as our Savior, we are always able to approach the throne of grace (Hebrews 4:14–16). Jude verse 24 promises that Jesus "is able to keep you from stumbling, and to make you stand in the presence of His glory blameless with great joy." You don't have to feel shame or unworthiness before the Father—Jesus took care of your shame on the cross. He is your adequacy. Of course,

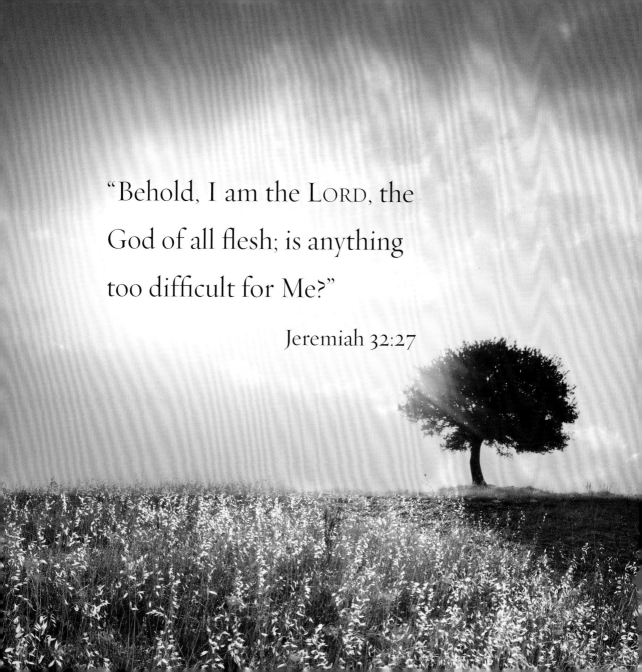

"Behold, I am the LORD, the God of all flesh; is anything too difficult for Me?"

Jeremiah 32:27

No matter how complicated, confusing, untenable, or overwhelming the trials you face, the living Lord is greater and can lead you to victory in them.

you should always repent of your sins, but that is to keep your fellowship with God unhindered, not so you can earn His approval.

Second, understand that as well as being omnipotent, omniscient, and omnipresent, the Father is also *omnibenevolent*, which means He is unconditional and perfect in His love for you. The Lord's love isn't based on what you do—it is based on His own unfailing character (1 John 4:8–10). The Father is completely kind and compassionate toward you because He cannot be otherwise—it is who He is. And as we just saw in Romans 8:38–39, absolutely nothing can separate us from His love.

So there is no need to wonder if the Lord is *willing* to help you—He is! Romans 8:31–32 declares, "What then shall we say to these things? If God is for us, who is against us? He who did not spare His own Son, but delivered Him over for us all, how will He not also with Him freely give us all things?"

Friend, God is not only prepared to help you but is actively calling you to cast "all your anxiety on Him, because He cares for you" (1 Peter 5:7). So if you are wondering if you can trust the Giver of this great gift of prayer . . . if He can truly help you . . . and if He is truly willing to help you . . . know for certain that the answer is unquestionably and resoundingly "Yes!" to all three questions!

The One who beckons you to His throne is worthy of your attention. Whereas earthly help will often fail you, He absolutely *never* will.

Lord Jesus, You are the One I need. Thank You for this great gift of prayer in which I can know You, experience Your presence, and receive Your aid.

Oh Lord, You are God! You are omniscient—knowing and understanding every working of everything in all creation. You are omnipresent—going where I cannot go and raising solutions I don't even realize exist. You are omnipotent—accomplishing all I am powerless to achieve in my strength. And You are loving—always providing what is most beneficial for me.

You are the sovereign, everlasting King of kings and Lord of lords. And You love me. You are not only able to help me but are always willing to deliver me. I have absolutely no reason to fear. You will not fail or forsake me. No one who trusts in You is ever put to shame.

Thank You, Father, for being greater than all my troubles and always helping me. I can always count on You!

In Your holy name I pray, Jesus. Amen.

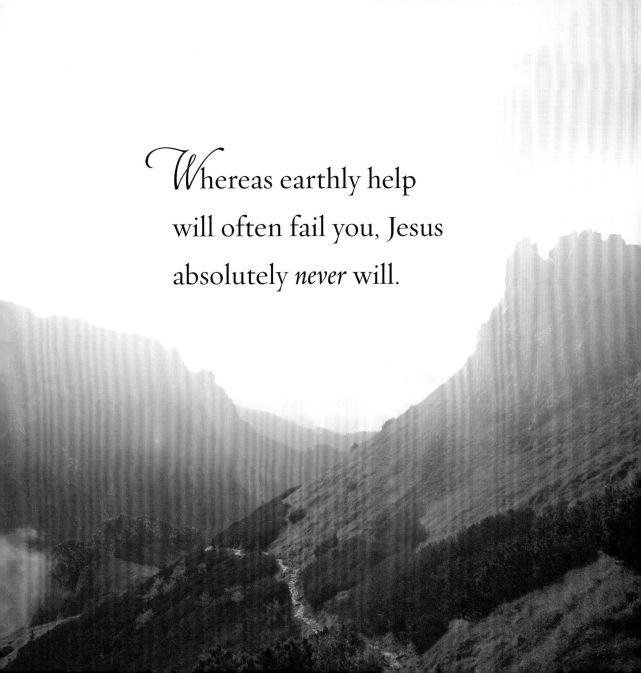

Whereas earthly help
will often fail you, Jesus
absolutely *never* will.

4

GETTING TO
KNOW THE GIVER

Who exactly is this God who created the heavens and the earth and who is on the other end of your conversation with Him? *How* you see Him is exceedingly important to your relationship with Him and the quality and impact of your life. Time in prayer helps you to know Him—who He is, His character, how He interacts with you. Not only do you understand His love *for you* but your love *for Him* increases as you know Him.

Think about it—your opinion of God influences your attitude when you are talking to Him. If you have a low view of the Father—thinking He is not actively engaged in your life or that He is in some way cruel—then you won't want to interact with Him. No one wants to spend time with people who are indifferent or mean.

Likewise, if you have an inadequate or negative view of who the Lord is, you will find yourself doubting and wavering during your most crucial moments. This is because you respond to God in proportion to what you believe about Him and how much you love Him. Your true view of Him is exposed during times of great pressure and trial.

But if you will read His Word and pray—not as a task or only as a discipline but as truly knowing God and building your intimate relationship with Him—you can sense how He is walking with you every step of the way. He begins to speak to your situation in a more profound and powerful manner than you ever expected.

So who is He? True, we just saw that the Lord is sovereign, omnipotent, omniscient, omnipresent, and omnibenevolent. He is God—the limitless, unwavering, and undeniable living King of all kings throughout eternity. He is *Yahweh*—the existing One and Great I Am. He is *Elohim*—the One who is infinite in power and absolutely faithful to keep His promises to you. He is *El Shaddai*—the almighty God, the all-sufficient One, the Most High over all, who is always victorious. Certainly, the One who helps you is awe-inspiring, impressive, capable, and deserving of complete respect.

But even those descriptions can appear cold and distant. Who is He personally? There are many names for God throughout Scripture that show how near He is to you and how tender He is toward you. The following is only a short list, but you can see His heart in them:

- *Yahweh Rohi*—the Lord your Shepherd (Psalm 23) and your Good Shepherd (John 10:14), who feeds you, tenderly cares for you, gently leads you, fiercely protects you, lays down His life for you, and makes sure you have no need.

- *El Roi* (Genesis 16:13)—He is the God who sees you—yes, all of you. From the struggles you face each and every day, to why they hurt so much, He knows you better than you know yourself. He sees your worth, and He loves you even when everyone else either can't understand you or seems to abandon you. In prayer, He reveals things about you even you didn't know were there in order to help you.

You respond to God in proportion to what you believe about Him and how much you love Him.

- *Yahweh Rapha* (Exodus 15:26) and the Great Physician (Mark 2:17)—the One who heals you both inside and out. As you pray, He mends those deep inner wounds and repairs their outward effects. That is His interest, friend—to heal you and lead you to true freedom from sin, not to harm you.
- *Yahweh Yireh* (Genesis 22:9–14)—your perfect Provider, who perceives your needs and faithfully supplies what will truly fulfill them. As you pray, the immensity of what you require melts away because you know who helps you—and He always has more than enough to supply whatever comes.

The Lord your God loves you. And His love for you is not like most human love—moody, unpredictable, self-serving, and contingent on your response. His tenderness toward you is based on His holy character—which is unwavering, sacrificial, unchanging, completely trustworthy, and committed to providing the very best for you. In fact, 1 John 4:8 explains that love is His very nature: "God is love." In other words, He cannot cease to care for you, because in order to do so, He would have to stop being Himself. Likewise, your heavenly Father won't love you more when you're obedient or less when you're sinful, because His affection is based on His unchanging disposition—not on your worthiness.

This is what time in prayer reveals to you—that you can truly count on God to help you. He is there for you. He is loving and faithful. He never abandons or rejects you. You never have to worry about Him saying one thing and doing another or acting in a harmful way toward you. Instead, you can count on the wonderful assurances He gives you every day of your life.

There was a time in my own life when I wrestled with knowing Jesus better and understanding how much He cared about me. Although everything else in my life seemed to be going well, I struggled inwardly. I called my four closest friends, who were all godly men, and said, "God is trying to teach me something, but I don't know what it is, and I need your help to figure it out. Here's what I want to do: I will tell you everything that I know about myself—good, bad, and indifferent. Then I would like the four of you to confer about what I should do. Whatever you agree to tell me, I'll do it. I know you're all listening to God."

We started about two o'clock in the afternoon and talked until ten o'clock that first night. After they went to bed, I wrote out seventeen legal-sized pages of experiences from my life I didn't want to forget to tell them.

The next day, we conversed for several more hours. Finally, one of the men said, "Charles, put your head on the table and close your eyes." I did. Quietly, he asked me, "Imagine your father just picked you up in his arms and held you. What do you feel?" He knew that my father died when I was nine months old and that his loss had a tremendous impact on my life. Immediately, I burst into tears, and I continued weeping for a long time. Still, I did not understand what was causing so much emotion. He asked me again, "What do you feel, Charles?"

The feelings were so overpowering, it was a long time before I could answer him. At last I replied, "I felt hugged, like I was warm and secure. I felt . . . loved." I realized that until that day, I had never really experienced God's love—not the unconditional and tender care of a Father as He seeks the absolute best for His children (1 John 3:1). I had told others about His love but had never truly sensed it like that myself. That day changed my life. The time with my four friends transformed my ministry and my life; the Father's love had become real to me and extremely powerful.

God knows you better than you know yourself. He sees your worth, and He loves you even when everyone else either can't understand you or seems to abandon you.

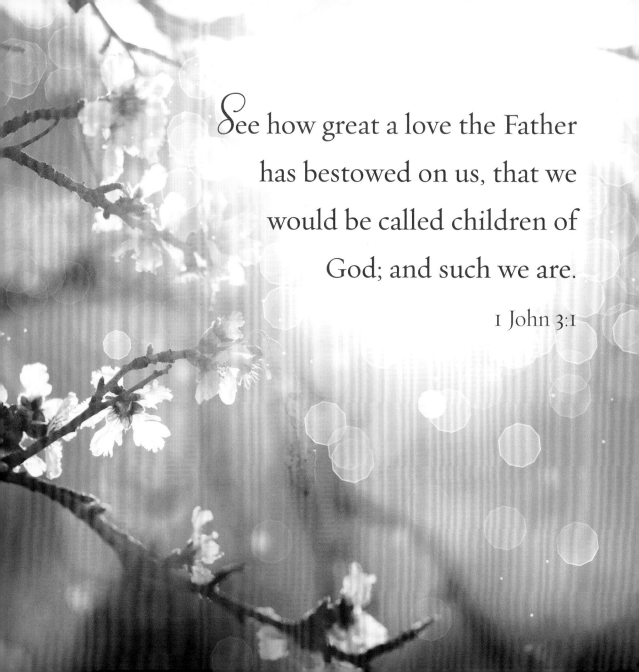

See how great a love the Father has bestowed on us, that we would be called children of God; and such we are.

1 John 3:1

I challenge you to do the same: put your head down and imagine the Father holding you. You may be surprised by the emotions you feel. You may, as I did, realize His overwhelming love for you. It is possible that you feel like pushing Him away because you do not really trust Him. A sense of conviction may come over you due to some unconfessed sin. You may realize that you've been running away from Him all your life when all you've wanted is to feel safe in your heavenly Father's arms.

Whatever the case, be still and allow God to deal with whatever emotions and issues arise. Do not fear. He is good, kind, and willing to teach you what to do. After all, this is the very foundation of prayer—understanding the great love He has for you, truly knowing Him, and allowing Him to lead you in a very personal way. Being still in His awesome embrace, knowing you are secure, realizing how deeply and eternally you're loved by your Creator, and receiving His perfect guidance are the great gifts of prayer.

The Father can remove any encumbrance you have to knowing Him, and He can draw you into a much deeper, more intimate relationship than you have ever known.

As I said at the beginning of the previous chapter, what makes prayer so powerful is the One with whom you are speaking. Fully embrace the fact that He is the infinite, inscrutable, invincible, and incontrovertible supreme Lord of all lords, who has utter power over every aspect of our universe and beyond. But even more than that, be aware of His love for you and live in the light of that truth.

He not only is worthy of your trust but also loves you unconditionally and wants to show you life at its best. Allow Him to reveal Himself to you.

Father, how very grateful I am for Your lovingkindness in allowing me to know You personally and to receive Your great love for me. I praise You, sovereign Lord of heaven and earth, the great and awesome God, for never failing to keep all of Your promises to those who love and obey You. But even more, I rest in Your arms as my Father—as the One who loves me most, guides me best, and is everything I need.

Yahweh Rohi, Jesus my Good Shepherd, thank You for caring for me so tenderly and laying down Your life for me. El Roi, thank You for seeing me—both my struggles and my potential—and for always being with me. Yahweh Rapha, my Great Physician, thank You for healing me inside and out—setting me free from the wounds in my heart as well as the sin that keeps me in bondage. And Yahweh Yireh, my perfect Provider, thank You for meeting my needs and faithfully supplying what will fulfill them. I never need to fear, because You are the One who helps me no matter what may come.

Lord, I recall the promise You made to me through the prophet Jeremiah: "You will seek Me and find Me when you search for Me with all your heart" (29:13). I pray that I can know You better and love You more through prayer. Lead me, Father. Help me to know You. And may I honor and glorify You today and every day. In Jesus' holy and wonderful name I pray. Amen.

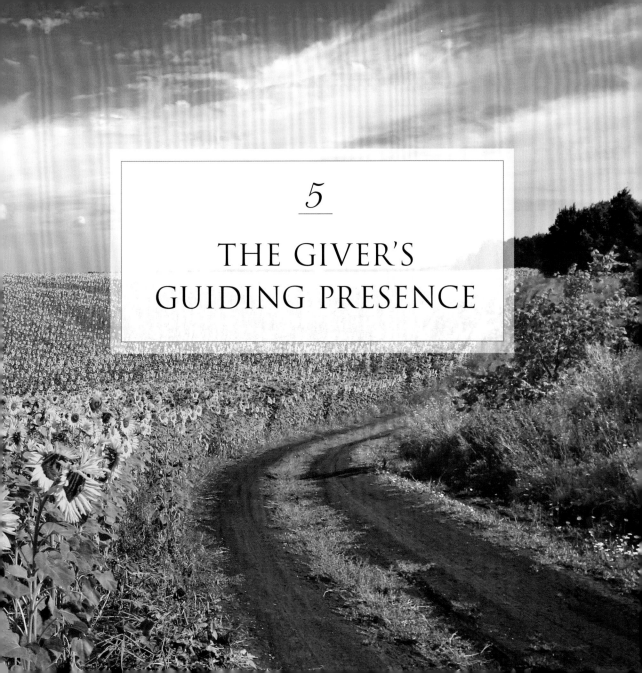

5

THE GIVER'S GUIDING PRESENCE

$\mathcal{S}$o far, we have focused on the fact that prayer offers us an awesome opportunity to know God, who always helps us. But often that is not really what is driving our prayers.

There are things we need, answers we long for, and problems that require wisdom that drive us to our knees. We need the help of the One described in the previous chapters. Perhaps we have claimed the awesome promises of Scripture:

- "Ask, and it will be given to you; seek, and you will find; knock, and it will be opened to you. For everyone who asks receives, and he who seeks finds, and to him who knocks it will be opened" (Matthew 7:7–8).
- "My God will supply all your needs according to His riches in glory in Christ Jesus" (Philippians 4:19).
- "If any of you lacks wisdom, let him ask of God, who gives to all generously and without reproach, and it will be given to him" (James 1:5).

We know God loves us and wants to deliver us.

The Spirit also helps our weakness; for we do not know how to pray as we should, but the Spirit Himself intercedes for us with groanings too deep for words; and He who searches the hearts knows what the mind of the Spirit is, because He intercedes for the saints according to the will of God.

Romans 8:26–27

However, we also know the Lord has requirements for us—and that's where we have trouble. For example, the admonition of 1 John 5:14 reminds us, "This is the confidence which we have before Him, that, if we ask anything *according to His will*, He hears us" (emphasis mine).

So yes, God *will* help us, but the glaring stipulation is there—*if we ask according to His will.*

Therefore, how can you know for certain that your prayer requests are pleasing to the Father? How can you be sure that what you're asking is right and according to His will?

These are the questions about prayer I hear most often. It can be discouraging if you aren't sure your request is compatible with God's plan. This can be especially true when you pray and pray but it seems as though the Lord's answers are delayed. Your troubles and needs continue to grow, and you may wonder if He hears you at all.

Have you ever felt this way? Have you ever been so encumbered by troubles that hopelessness overcomes you? You just don't know what to say to God. Perhaps you feel as if you don't know how to express the full depth of what you feel in an accurate and reverent manner. You may even be so exhausted, heartbroken, or discouraged that you don't really know what you need and aren't sure how to ask the Father to help you.

If so, then realize that God has given you an awesome gift by sending a Helper to dwell in you. The Lord has shown His love for you by giving you an awesome prayer Partner to accompany you throughout your life and in your most confusing moments.

The apostle Paul explained, "The Spirit also helps our weakness; for we do not know how to pray as we should, but the Spirit Himself intercedes for us with groanings too deep for words; and He who searches the hearts knows what the mind of the Spirit is, because He intercedes for the saints according to the will of God" (Romans 8:26–27).

God understood you would feel weak in prayer—that at times you wouldn't even really know why your heart is as heavy, burdened, tired, or full of pain as it is. So He has given you His Holy Spirit, who is like an ambassador who faithfully conveys the Father's will to you in a way you'll understand and who represents you before God in a manner worthy of His righteous name.

What does the Spirit do? He guides you so that the following six aspects of answered prayer are met in you:

The Lord has shown His love for you by giving you an awesome prayer Partner to accompany you throughout your life and in your most confusing moments.

1. *Right Relationship*—In Psalm 66:18 we read, "If I regard wicked-ness in my heart, the Lord will not hear." In other words, sin can block our prayers to God. This does not mean every time we make a mistake or stumble spiritually the Lord refuses to hear our petitions. Rather, our heavenly Father understands the fears, wounds, weaknesses, and difficulties we face. He also wants to free us from them. So the Holy Spirit will speak to us about the areas that are blocking the Lord's holy power in our lives. He teaches us to live according to the principles of His Word and according to His guidance so we can experience His best.

2. *Right Heart*—What is your true motive in approaching the throne of grace? Is it getting your way or knowing the Father and experiencing His awesome presence? Do you approach Him with a grocery list of requests or to understand His plan for your life? Understand that Jesus has expressed His goal for a relationship with you. He said, "Let your light so shine before men in such a way that they may see your good works, and glorify your Father who is in heaven" (Matthew 5:16). That is His ultimate purpose for you—to shine through you so

others will know Him. Therefore, the Holy Spirit will cleanse your heart of the things that would exalt you but would bring dishonor to Christ—convicting you of what does not glorify the Father.

Does that mean you can still pray for your daily needs—such as getting over a cold, having enough money for the light bill, or desiring for a relationship to be restored? Can a prayer for something seemingly unrelated to the kingdom of God give glory to Him? Of course it can. But we must be willing to see our requests as both a way to know the Lord better and a testimony to others of His faithfulness. In this way, God receives praise out of any prayer He answers. When people hear of a specific request being met, their faith is strengthened. So when we set our sights in prayer on knowing the Father and giving Him glory—rather than just getting what we're asking for—He delights in answering our prayers.

3. *Right Attitude*—The book of James describes the attitude we are to have when making requests: "Ask in faith without any doubting, for the one who doubts is like the surf of the sea, driven and tossed by the wind" (James 1:6). Doubt and prayer

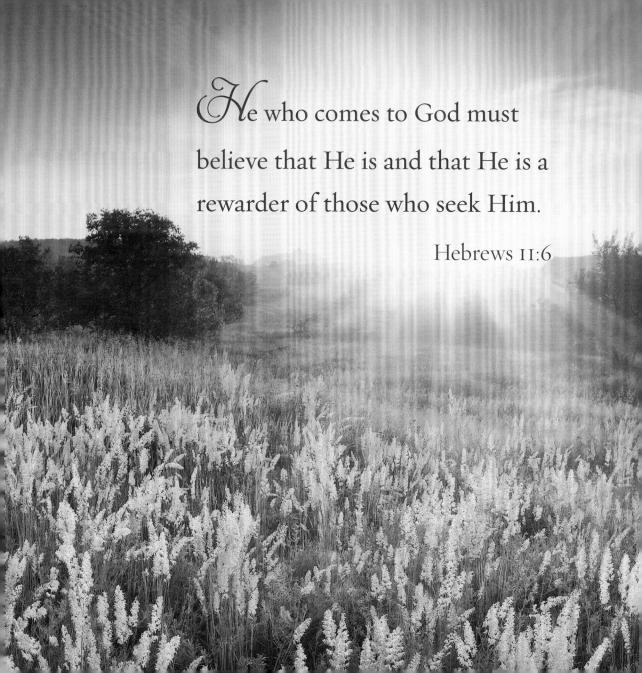

He who comes to God must believe that He is and that He is a rewarder of those who seek Him.

Hebrews 11:6

do not mix. A man whose faith wavers in prayer is a "double-minded man" and is "unstable in all his ways" (James 1:8). He is unstable not only in his prayer life but in all his ways. What then is the right attitude? What is this faith we are to have? Hebrews 11:6 explains, "He who comes to God must believe that He is and that He is a rewarder of those who seek Him." In other words, we must truly believe the Lord will answer us and that He will do what is in our best interest.

So the Holy Spirit will allow circumstances to arise that you do not understand, and He will sometimes answer in a manner that is—for the moment—confusing to you. But He is doing so for your welfare, not to hurt you—to build your trust in God, who sees beyond you and will often work in the unseen. Jesus summed it up like this: "I say to you, all things for which you pray and ask, believe that you have received them, and they will be granted you" (Mark 11:24). Faith is the capacity to trust God's word above what you see and treat His promises as if they have already been fulfilled for you (Isaiah 55:10–11). Because then you can step out and obey Him, trusting He will always lead you in the right way (Proverbs 3:5–6).

4. *Right Method*—This means *how* we go to the Lord in prayer. When many of us pray, we add "in Jesus' name" to the end of our prayers either as a habit or to claim Christ's promise of John 14:14: "If you ask Me anything in My name, I will do it." But praying in Jesus' name is more than a phrase we add to a prayer; it is the character of the prayer itself. To appeal to God in His name means that we are asking for what Jesus would request if He were in our circumstances.

   This may seem too difficult or unattainable to you. How can you possibly know what Jesus would pray? Yet that is another reason the Holy Spirit works in you—to give you the "mind of Christ" (1 Corinthians 2:16). He not only lives through you but intercedes through you as well. He uncovers your true needs and the real issues that God is addressing in you.

5. *Right Tool*—Because you have been made spiritually alive in Christ, you now have spiritual challenges that will surface. At times, these matters and battles will be easy to discern, but at other times, they will be disguised in ordinary troubles. For example, you may think some irritation or frustration you are experiencing is due to your circumstances or relationships, but

The Father longs for you to seek His face, not just His hand. He has sent you a Helper to teach you how to communicate with Him.

it really originates with a spiritual source—either bondage in you or spiritual warfare. Therefore, one of the roles of the Holy Spirit is to help you understand where your problems are coming from and give you the right tools—such as Scripture and wisdom from above (James 3:13–18)—to overcome them.

Ephesians 6:12 reveals, "Our struggle is not against flesh and blood, but against the rulers, against the powers, against the world forces of this darkness, against the spiritual forces of wickedness in the heavenly places." The Holy Spirit will give you the right tools and weapons to fight the true enemy you're facing (1 Corinthians 10:3–5).

6. *Right Request*—This all leads up to the Holy Spirit helping you to make the right request, assisting you in asking God for His provision according to His will (1 John 5:14). He helps you to have a vibrant relationship with Christ, a clean heart in knowing Him, godly motives in your petitions, effective methods in asking, and powerful tools for understanding your true needs so that you can express your desire to Him. He also communicates God's will to you and helps you to hear and accept the Father's answer to the cries of your heart.

As I've said, God loves you and wants to meet your needs. In fact, He wants to give you the desires of your heart (Psalm 37:4). But the Father longs for you to seek His face, not just His hand. He has sent you a Helper to teach you how to communicate with Him and pray according to His will.

Because the Holy Spirit lives within you, you have the Lord's constant presence and guidance to prompt you in the way you should go (1 Corinthians 3:16; 6:19; 2 Corinthians 6:16). You don't have to struggle with knowing what to say to the Father or wish you had a better vocabulary to address Him. You don't have to wonder whether God understands what you mean or if you have asked for the wrong thing. Your personal prayer Partner is always with you and helps you fellowship with the Father. The true question is whether you'll listen to Him and accept the help He gives you to pray according to His will.

So don't fear whether God will acknowledge the cries of your heart. Rather, listen to His Holy Spirit and allow Him to transform your petitions into acceptable and pleasing sacrifices (Revelation 5:8; 8:3–4).

Holy Spirit, how grateful I am for Your indwelling, unshakable presence in my life! Thank You for teaching me and helping me as I communicate with the Father. Thank You for searching me and freeing me from the fears, wounds, weaknesses, and difficulties that are in me so I can have a right relationship with God.

Certainly, You are teaching me to have faith, reminding me of God's work in the unseen, revealing how to pray with the character of Christ, and equipping me with the right tools for everything I face. Thank You for bringing to mind Scripture to guide me and helping to address the areas that You are transforming by Your grace.

I will not fear coming before the great throne of grace to participate in this great gift of prayer, because I know You are with me, Holy Spirit. Help me to hear You and submit to Your promptings. In Jesus' name and according to His matchless character I pray. Amen.

THE BENEFITS
of the GIFT

The most powerful thing you can do—the most awesome privilege you have in this life—is to talk to the heavenly Father about anything in your heart.

You can touch anyone, anywhere in the world, through your prayers, no matter the circumstance.

You can move mountains, change nations, and overcome any problem as you talk with the Lord.

6

PRAYER IS AN EMPOWERING GIFT

*P*rayer is certainly an amazing gift because of *who* we get to know and how He teaches us to walk with Him. However, it is also an astounding blessing because of what He does for us.

Never is this more apparent than when we experience the full weight of our inadequacies. Life presents problems and tests that are much more than we can handle on our own. We may feel overcome by our difficulties and find ourselves thinking, *This challenge is much greater than I am, and I don't know what to do. I need help.* It is then—and sometimes only then—that we turn to our loving Father in prayer.

I experienced this after graduating from the University of Richmond when I went to Southwestern Baptist Theological Seminary in Fort Worth, Texas. I was about halfway through the three-year program, and I was beginning to think about my future and was completely overwhelmed by all the unknowns. It was one of those nights when I longed to pick up the phone and call the earthly father I never knew and tell him what I was thinking. I wondered what was ahead, how I would know what to do, and how I would always be sure to honor God with my decisions. I needed assurance that I was taking the right path—that I wasn't headed for failure and disappointment. The more I thought about it, the more impossible everything seemed.

"Not by might nor by power, but by My Spirit," says the LORD of hosts.

Zechariah 4:6

So I knelt to pray. As I did, I had a very strong sense of the Lord's presence. I did not hear His voice audibly, but His message to me could not have been clearer. He said, "Whatever you accomplish in life will not depend on your education, your talent, or your skill. I have a plan for you, but you will only accomplish it on your knees in complete surrender to Me." I have never forgotten that night. And throughout my life, I have started and ended my days on my knees before God to talk to Him and to listen to what else He has to say.

What the Father communicated to me was the same message that we read in Zechariah 4:6: "'Not by might nor by power, but by My Spirit,' says the LORD of hosts." As I said in the previous chapter, the Holy Spirit teaches us the Father's will, how to listen to Him, and how to have an intimate relationship with Him. But He also trains and empowers us to fulfill God's plans for our lives with strength and wisdom from above.

In a similar manner, your obstacles and trials may drive you to your knees before almighty God. And perhaps you've noticed that the more inadequate, perplexed, and overwhelmed you feel, the more motivated you are to pray. I know I certainly am. But also realize that understanding how vastly insufficient you are for the problems you face is actually a blessing. This is because when you humble yourself—admitting you need the Father's help—you are finally in the exact position necessary to receive all the power, energy, wisdom, and strength you need to conquer those troubles successfully. You are able to experience the awesome provision and victory that God has for you because you're ready to obey whatever He commands.

The principle here is this: *you and I stand tallest and strongest on our knees.* That is, when we are overwhelmed by troubles, there is one course of action we can take every time that we know is absolutely right—and that is to engage in the gift of prayer. We see this principle throughout Scripture, especially in the life of Nehemiah.

It had been 140 years since the Babylonians had destroyed Jerusalem—tearing down its walls, destroying the temple, and carrying the people of Judah into captivity (2 Kings 25). Although the Persians had defeated the Babylonians and had allowed the Jews to return to Jerusalem (Ezra 1), Nehemiah, a godly man and cupbearer to King Artaxerxes of Persia, received word that things were not going well in the city. He wrote,

> Some men from Judah came; and I asked them concerning the Jews who had escaped and had survived the captivity, and

$\mathcal{T}$he Holy Spirit trains
and empowers us to fulfill
God's plans for our lives
with strength from above.

about Jerusalem. They said to me, "The remnant there in the province who survived the captivity are in great distress and reproach, and the wall of Jerusalem is broken down and its gates are burned with fire."

When I heard these words, I sat down and wept and mourned for days; and I was fasting and praying before the God of heaven. (Nehemiah 1:2–4)

As you can imagine, this man of God was heartbroken. Although it had been several decades since the Jews had returned to Jerusalem, they were unsuccessful in rebuilding its walls. It was a terrible situation. How would God's people ever be reestablished in the land of their inheritance if they could not even fortify their main city? Nehemiah understood that the situation needed to change immediately.

But what could one man do? How could one person take on the tremendous task of refortifying such an important city? If anyone had a right to feel inadequate, disheartened, perplexed, and overwhelmed, it was Nehemiah. But instead of giving in to discouragement, Nehemiah prayed. He realized that if he were going to succeed, it would be in the Lord's way and time.

Scripture testifies that the Father did an awesome work in Nehemiah's life. The Lord not only gave Nehemiah incredible favor with King Artaxerxes but also protected him from all the enemies that had previously prevented Jerusalem from rising again. And the walls that had lain in ruin for more than 140 years were rebuilt in just fifty-two days under Nehemiah's leadership (Nehemiah 6:15–16).

Only the Father could empower Nehemiah to do that. But what I would like you to realize today is that the same God who helped Nehemiah is with you in everything you face. He can work through your life in the most awesome way, if you will allow Him. All it takes is going before the Lord in humble, trusting, and believing prayer.

When you face a challenge that is much greater than your capacity to handle, or you are confused about what to do, understand that you have an excellent opportunity to see how tall and strong you stand on your knees. Invite God to exercise His power in your life, give you wisdom, and provide for your needs. Humble yourself before God and recognize Him as your sovereign Lord. Just as He did with Nehemiah, He will surely help you triumph over the tremendous obstacles you face and reveal Himself to you in a wonderful way.

Father, how grateful I am that where I am weak, You are strong; where I fall short, You show forth abundantly. Lord, You know where I feel inadequate—where my talent, resources, energy, wisdom, and strength are just not enough for the obstacles before me. I thank You that You've brought these circumstances into my life to show me who You are. You have allowed them so that I will bow in prayer and seek You and so I will see You for who You truly are.

Whenever I am afraid or feel hopeless, remind me to look to You, because You are more than able, Lord! You are the God who can do all things—the only Ruler of heaven and earth. In Your hand is all creation, and nothing can stand against You. You open doors that no one can close. You supply all I need in ways I cannot even think to ask or imagine. You are faithful and true; the King of kings and the Lord of lords; the omnipotent Sovereign over all that exists; the One who provides for, protects, strengthens, directs, and establishes me. I will trust You in my inadequacies because I know Your power and grace are perfected and exalted through my weaknesses. Thank You, Lord, for the precious gift of prayer that allows me to take hold of You.

In the empowering and all-sufficient name of Jesus I pray. Amen.

You and I stand
tallest and strongest
on our knees.

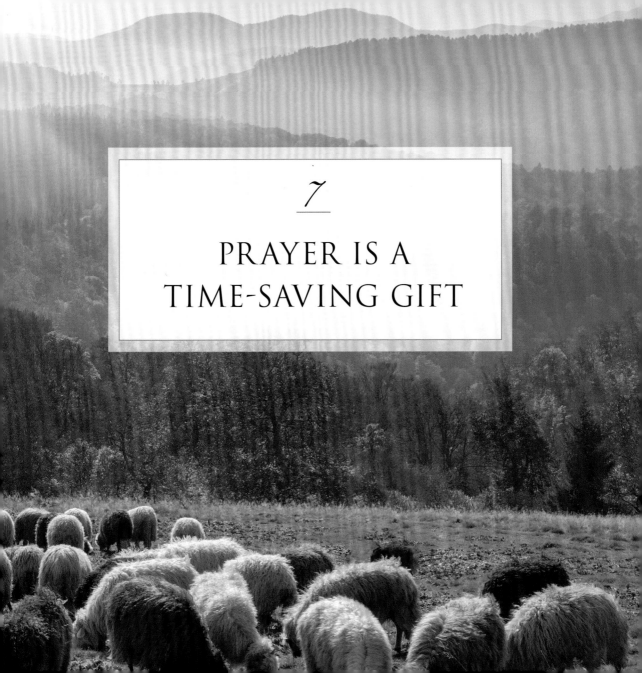

7

PRAYER IS A
TIME-SAVING GIFT

The title of this chapter may be surprising to you. Most people, at one time or another, have thought, *I am just too busy to pray.* How in the world can prayer *save* time if it takes time to pray? In fact, prayer may be the first thing you cut when your schedule fills up.

But do you ever wonder where all your time has gone? In all your efforts to be efficient and a wise steward of time, its swift passing can surprise us. It could be you have deadlines that are pressing, and you are uncertain how to fulfill your responsibilities. Maybe your loved ones are growing older more quickly than you anticipated, and you wonder how you can make the most of every moment with them. Or perhaps you are the one getting older and you've not achieved all you wished to accomplish by this point in your life.

Whatever the case, you recognize the reality of Psalm 144:4: "Man is like a mere breath; his days are like a passing shadow." In the grand scheme of things, you haven't had as secure a handle on your time as you've hoped.

A dear friend of mine experienced this when he was diagnosed with cancer. Understanding how precious time is, he told me, "Every morning since the doctor gave me the news, I wake up and the first thing I do is thank God for another day and ask Him to show me how to spend it wisely." Everything changed for my friend the moment he realized how valuable every minute is.

We are sensible to do the same—recognizing our time as a gift from the Father and making the most of the days we're given. Whether it is showing those we love that we care, meeting steep deadlines, or pursuing goals the Lord has called us to achieve, we must be sure we're investing our time prudently and not wasting it.

*T*each us to number our days, that we may present to You a heart of wisdom.

Psalm 90:12

But how do we do so? How can we safeguard our time and make sure we're not squandering it? I can say without a shadow of a doubt that the most important thing we can do to ensure that our lives are productive is to listen to God. As we've seen in the previous chapters, the Lord is absolutely wise and omniscient, and He always knows the best path for our lives.

This is why I read the following portion of Psalm 119 almost every day. It reminds me that I belong to the Father, I need Him, and He is the One who must guide my footsteps.

> I am Your servant; give me understanding,
> That I may know Your testimonies.
> It is time for the LORD to act,
> For they have broken Your law.
> Therefore I love Your commandments
> Above gold, yes, above fine gold.
> Therefore I esteem right all Your precepts concerning
>   everything,
> I hate every false way.

Your testimonies are wonderful;
Therefore my soul observes them.
The unfolding of Your words gives light;
It gives understanding to the simple.
I opened my mouth wide and panted,
For I longed for Your commandments.
Turn to me and be gracious to me,
After Your manner with those who love Your name.
Establish my footsteps in Your word,
And do not let any iniquity have dominion over me.
(Psalm 119:125–133)

Why is talking to the Father such a powerful way to guard our time? Here are ten reasons why prayer is life's greatest time-saver and always our most productive course of action:

- Listening to God keeps you from making wrong decisions that would have negative, long-range repercussions or would cause you costly delays.

- Remaining constant in your conversation with the Father reveals open doors of opportunity that you may never have seen otherwise.
- The Holy Spirit will remind you to act on important decisions and activities that you may forget or wrongly consider insignificant.
- Through intimate communion with the Savior, worry, anxiety, and fretting—three terrible time wasters—can be eliminated because you grow in assurance of His character. Instead, you are filled with His hope and peace.
- When emergencies arise, you can receive clear, timely direction from the Lord through prayer, which eliminates confusion.
- You receive God's viewpoint about your situation, so you can see through surface issues to what's really happening.
- Even if you should start down the wrong path out of ignorance, God can get you back on track as you spend time in His presence and listen to Him.
- Time with the Savior sharpens your discernment and can help you avoid wasteful activities and relationships that achieve nothing. The Lord prevents you from being distracted by the wrong things and getting sidetracked.

*E*very morning, thank God for another day and ask Him to show you how to spend it wisely.

- Likewise, committing your ways to the Lord through the gift of prayer helps you discern the difference between *busyness* and true *fruitfulness*—making you more efficient, effective, and productive.
- Finally, as we saw in the previous chapter, your communion with the Father gives you energy—enabling you to accomplish the great things He calls you to more quickly than apart from Him.

As you can see, there are many valuable, time-saving benefits to prayer. But friend, if you're too busy to pray or wait for God to reveal His will, then one thing is certain—you're headed for trouble.

We invest our time based on how much we value someone or something—and there is nothing more valuable than your intimate relationship with God. You can never afford to be too busy for Him. Psalm 90:12 says, "Teach us to number our days, that we may present to You a heart of wisdom." God is the One who shows you both the importance of your time and how to be most effective in investing it.

If you are wrestling with the reality of the days, weeks, and years that have passed, remember that the most significant and most effective thing you can do is listen to God by reading His Word and spending time with Him in intimate communion.

Father, I confess I have not always put You first when it comes to the issue of time. I realize time is a tool in Your hand and that You have a wisdom about it that escapes me. You see from beginning to end, while I have only a limited view of the past and the moment I am in. Thank You for the great gift of prayer that You work through to make my time effective, meaningful, and fruitful.

Lord, teach me what is important in Your sight. You see the future and what is truly vital for it. Help me to walk in Your timing and ways. Keep me from making wrong decisions, show me Your open doors of opportunity, remind me of what I need to do, eliminate wasteful and counterproductive time eaters from my life, and help me to remain patient and hopeful in the delays. Likewise, Father, in these areas where I feel like I am running out of time, please lead me. You know how to make the most of the moments—to invest them wisely in a manner that will honor You and bring peace to my soul. Teach me to number my days, hours, minutes, and seconds wisely, that I may walk in Your will and experience life at its best and most fruitful.

I pray this in the eternal name of Jesus. Amen.

*T*alking to the Father is the most powerful way to guard our time and guarantee that it is used effectively.

8

PRAYER IS A
PEACE-GIVING GIFT

*M*any decades ago, one of my college friends gave me a small picture that has meant a great deal to me. There is nothing remarkable about it from an artistic standpoint, but it has given me great comfort during some important times nonetheless.

In fact, not long ago, I asked the Lord for direction about a difficult situation. I felt very alone. Confused and unable to discuss my difficulties with others, I got down on my knees in a quiet room and cried out to God to help me, strengthen me, and change the situation that was causing me pain. I asked, "Father, please don't leave me like this. Show me what to do."

As I was praying, I looked up, and there was that picture. In it, the Lord Jesus is standing behind a young man, pointing out the right course for the fellow to take. The Master's hand is on his shoulder, as if saying, "I am with you always" (Matthew 28:20) and "This is the way, walk in it" (Isaiah 30:21).

In that instant, God showed me that He was in complete control of the situation and that He would help me get to the destination He planned for me. Like the young man in the picture, I needed to stay focused on the path that the Master was pointing me to. And

Be anxious for nothing, but in everything by prayer and supplication with thanksgiving let your requests be made known to God. And the peace of God, which surpasses all comprehension, will guard your hearts and your minds in Christ Jesus.

Philippians 4:6–7

if I would obey Him—even when the road seemed dark—He would certainly bless my faith in Him.

I tell you this because, inevitably, there will be times in your life when you just don't know what to do. You may feel overwhelmed by the questions that plague you and shut down—becoming paralyzed and unable to move forward. Or perhaps you lie awake at night, consumed by the details of your circumstances and rehearsing them repeatedly in the hope of making some sense of them. Either way, you feel trapped, because you have no idea how to proceed.

You will feel as if your anxiety is tearing you apart. And that is what fear does—it scatters your thoughts, pulling you in different directions with all the "what ifs." But this stands in direct opposition to what the Father desires for you.

Jesus said, "I have spoken to you, so that in Me you may have peace" (John 16:33). *Peace.* It is a word that in the Greek means "joined or bound together." For example, through Jesus' sacrifice on the cross, we can have peace—or be united—with Him and be fully reconciled to the Father (Colossians 1:20).

However, *peace* also means an internal sense of harmony and tranquility. Everything within us is calm—confident "that God causes all things to work together for good to those who love God, to those who are called according to His purpose" (Romans 8:28). It is Jesus' goal that we would possess the inward composure that comes from having a personal relationship with Him and enjoying His provision. And He has given us the gift of prayer for this purpose.

Philippians 4:6–7 promises, "Be anxious for nothing, but in everything by prayer and supplication with thanksgiving let your requests be made known to God. And the peace of God, which surpasses all comprehension, will guard your hearts and your minds in Christ Jesus." The word there for *guard* means to "garrison you about, hem you in, and protect by a military sentinel." As you exercise the gift of prayer and walk with God, He encompasses you as your Protector and Provider—and no one can break through His defenses. The Father encircles you with His own matchless presence, and the only way anything can get to you is if He Himself opens the door and allows it. That is the greatest security you and I could ever ask for.

Do you need peace in some area? Are you facing a situation that is confusing—that is tearing you apart? Do you lack a clear course of action?

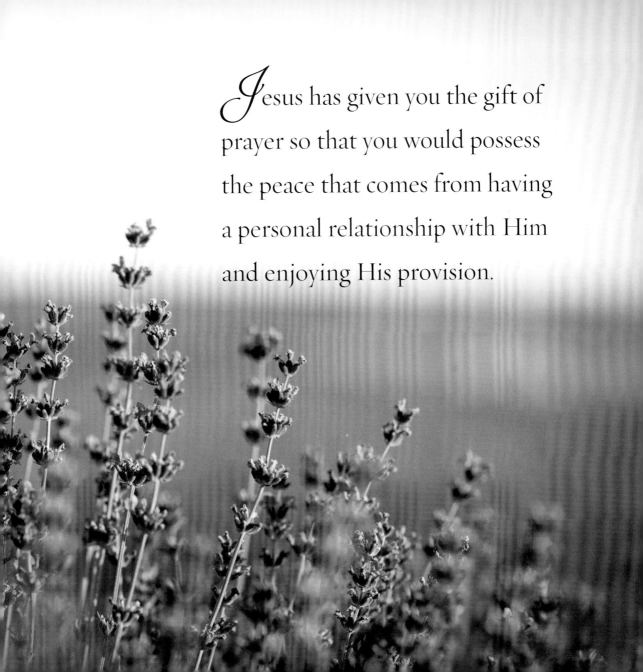

Jesus has given you the gift of prayer so that you would possess the peace that comes from having a personal relationship with Him and enjoying His provision.

*J*esus knows exactly what you really need and how to provide it in the most loving and edifying way possible. He is committed to seeing you become all He created you to be.

Jesus' hand is on your shoulder, and He's pointing you in the right direction—the right path for your life. Are you listening to Him and submitting to His guidance? Or are you living your life the way you want to—in your wisdom rather than His?

All of us need a reliable guide to instruct us, and none is more trustworthy than the Savior who laid down His life on our behalf. But perhaps you are unsure—can you truly trust the Lord with the situation that is currently causing you so much stress and anxiety? Here are two reasons why I am confident you can and should.

The first reason trusting Jesus to guide you will bring you peace is because you know He will never lead you astray. As I said previously, His character is above reproach. His comprehension of all things past, present, and future is beyond compare. He not only has the wisdom to counsel you, but He loves you and always has your best interest at heart. Deuteronomy 31:8 promises, "The Lord is the one who goes ahead of you; He will be with you. He will not fail you or forsake you. Do not fear or be dismayed." God will never mislead or abandon you, no matter what decision you must make. He will direct you in the best path possible if you will follow Him. If that doesn't give you peace, I don't know what will!

Second, trusting Jesus to guide you will bring you peace because He is leading you on a road that is unique to you. This world offers many one-size-fits-all solutions to our problems, and often they do not work or cause even more damage. But Jesus' knowledge of you is perfect—He understands your personality, strengths, weaknesses, joys, sorrows, needs, temptations, desires, and concerns. Also, He created you for a distinctive purpose. Ephesians 2:10 explains, "We are His workmanship, created in Christ Jesus for good works, which God prepared beforehand so that we would walk in them." When the Lord formed you, there were special assignments He planned for you to accomplish, which are tailor-made for your giftedness and temperament. Your being is satisfied, finds meaning, and is fulfilled in knowing Him and achieving those purposes.

This all means that the road you are to take must be specially crafted for you—specific to your makeup and to the reasons you were created as you were. This is why it is so important for God to set your course—because only your Lord and Savior knows your true potential, how to overcome the dangers ahead, and how to arrive at your destination in the safest and most effective way possible. And this is why His leadership should give you peace—He knows exactly what you really need and how to provide it in the most loving and edifying way possible. He is invested in you and is committed to seeing you become all He created you to be.

In Psalm 32:8, He promises, "I will instruct you and teach you in the way which you should go; I will counsel you with My eye upon you." Will you trust Him to do so? I hope you will. He knows exactly where you are, what you need to do in the situation you're facing, and how to get you to the wonderful destination He's planned for you. He is your Protector and Provider and has everything necessary to get you to the goal even when the path seems impossible. Only the Lord can meet those high standards that can ensure your peace.

Pray to Him and trust Him to be your leader in every situation, because surely He will bless you with His peace that transcends understanding as you follow Him.

Lord God, thank You so much for always being with me—for never leaving or abandoning me. I am so grateful that You are leading me through this great gift of prayer. Like a loving Father or a gentle Shepherd, You direct me on the path I need to take—to drive out sin, heal my wounds, develop my gifts, build my character, and teach me more about You. Thank You, Lord.

You encompass me as my perfect Protector and Provider—and no one can break through Your defenses. You guide me with Your hand on my shoulder and encircle me with Your own matchless presence. I thank You that the only way anything can get to me is if You allow it for my ultimate edification and benefit. What great tranquility that gives my heart—that all things will work together for my good!

You keep me secure in Your steadfast, unending, unshakable love. Thank You, Lord! There is no peace like the peace You give, Lord Jesus! In Your matchless name I pray. Amen.

"Peace I leave with you; My peace I give to you; not as the world gives do I give to you. Do not let your heart be troubled, nor let it be fearful."

John 14:27

9

PRAYER IS A TRANSFORMATIVE GIFT

hroughout my years in ministry, many people have asked for prayer for some problem or difficulty they are experiencing. Some individuals are specific about what they would like me to pray about. They share their hearts and detailed accounts of their struggles.

But often, people just say, "Pastor, would you pray for me?" They need God to intervene in a particular situation, relationship, or stronghold in their lives but feel uncomfortable expressing their feelings or failings. They just know they need the Father's help and guidance. Has this ever happened to you? Have you been asked to intercede for someone without knowing all the facts?

It is also possible the Lord has put someone on your heart, and you know that you need to lift that person up, but you have no idea why. It could even be that there is someone in your life who is struggling with issues of bondage and you just don't know how to help him or her anymore. Perhaps you've wondered, *How can I pray powerfully for that person when I don't know what to request? I know God understands all needs, but I want to pray in a manner that makes a difference. What do I do?*

You know Ephesians 6:18 (NLT) instructs, "Pray in the Spirit at all times and on every occasion. Stay alert and be persistent in your prayers for all believers everywhere." But how do you pray?

Thankfully, Scripture instructs you about how to intercede in these situations. And if you learn to pray this simple, life-changing prayer, you are guaranteed three things:

- First, God's Word promises that if you pray in faith and are consistent about it, the Father will work through your prayers in a powerful way.
- Second, you will be praying in perfect agreement with the will of God.
- Third, you know that His answer to this prayer is always "Yes!"

What is this life-changing prayer? It is found in Colossians 1:9–12:

We have not ceased to pray for you and to ask that you may be filled with the knowledge of His will in all spiritual wisdom and understanding, so that you will walk in a manner worthy of the Lord, to please Him in all respects, bearing fruit in every good work and increasing in the knowledge of God;

strengthened with all power, according to His glorious might, for the attaining of all steadfastness and patience; joyously giving thanks to the Father, who has qualified us to share in the inheritance of the saints in Light.

First, pray for the person to be filled with the knowledge of God's will (Colossians 1:9). There is no better, no safer place for anyone to be than in the center of the Father's will—trusting Jesus Christ as Savior, being transformed into His image, and obeying all His commands. No matter what decision that person must make or what obstacle he must face, when he knows and does the will of God, he takes the very best path possible for his life and will have everything necessary to succeed.

Second, pray that the person would walk in a manner worthy of the Lord (Colossians 1:10). As Christ's ambassador, your loved one has a responsibility to represent Him well to others—to live a life that honors Him in every way. This means that she is to be obedient to Jesus in conversation, conduct, and character. When you pray that she walks in a manner worthy of the Lord, you are praying that she will avoid temptation and stand strong for Him.

*P*ray in the Spirit at all times
and on every occasion. Stay alert
and be persistent in your prayers
for all believers everywhere.

Ephesians 6:18 NLT

Third, pray that the person would bear fruit in every good work (Colossians 1:10). A believer's life should have an eternal impact, and your friend should be influencing those around him for the sake of God's kingdom. Is he? Pray that he would submit to the Lord, be a light to those around him, and give the Father all the glory in every circumstance.

Fourth, pray for the person to increase in the knowledge of God (Colossians 1:10). Believers are to be constantly maturing in their faith and being transformed into the image of Christ. Pray that in every blessing or difficulty, instead of panicking or seeking her own solutions, your loved one will trust in God and ask Him, "Lord, what would You have me learn in this situation?"

Fifth, pray for the person to be strengthened with all power (Colossians 1:11). Ask God to empower your friend as he seeks Him wholeheartedly, knowing that the Lord is faithful to assume full responsibility for all his needs as he obeys Him.

Finally, joyously give thanks to the Father for the individual's life (Colossians 1:11–12). Thank God for all He is doing in and through your loved one—all the ways He is teaching and working through her. And especially praise Him that because she has trusted in Christ's death on the cross, her sins have been forgiven and she has a home in heaven forever.

Your heavenly Father will be faithful to hear your prayers and fulfill His promises. So never question whether your times with the Lord on behalf of others matter. They absolutely do. In fact, they will make more of a difference than you can possibly imagine.

So intercede for your friends and loved ones. Your prayers do not have to be specific, but they do need to be full of faith, consistent, and according to God's will. Thankfully, you can know that as you pray Colossians 1:9–12, the Father not only honors your prayers but answers "Yes!" to every one of them. Rejoice in the transformative gift of prayer.

Father, how grateful I am that I can talk to You about absolutely anything—including the needs of my family members, friends, coworkers, fellow believers, and acquaintances. I may not be able to help them, but I am thankful that through the awesome gift of prayer I can lift them up to You—and You can transform their lives in miraculous ways.

You know who is on my heart right now, Father. I pray that this individual would be filled with the knowledge of Your will, would walk in a manner worthy of You, would bear fruit in every good work, would increase in the knowledge of You, and would be strengthened with all Your power and wisdom to stand against sin and embrace who You created him or her to be. I give thanks to You, Father, for this person's life. I know You formed this precious individual with great purposes in mind—even if this person is far from those plans right now. But with You, Father, there is always hope! Transform this situation in the way only You can.

In Jesus' loving and life-changing name I pray. Amen.

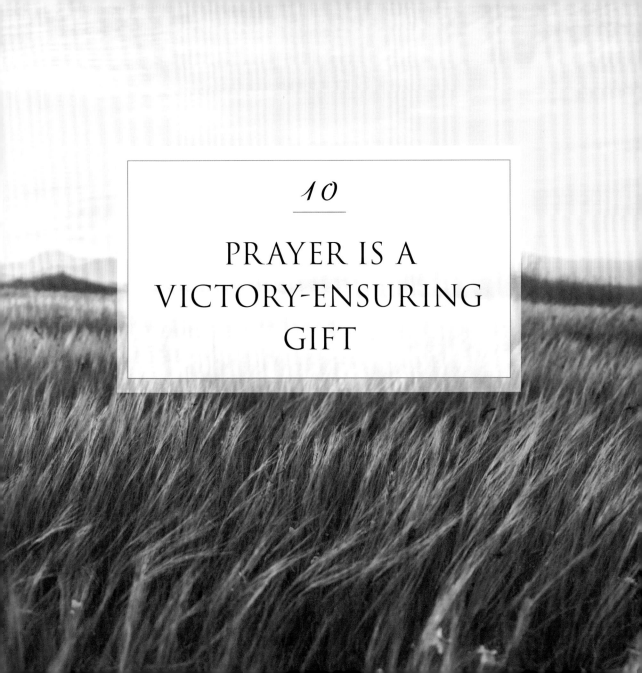

10

PRAYER IS A VICTORY-ENSURING GIFT

Have you ever experienced a battle so deep and overwhelming it felt as if everything in your life were against you? Do you, in a very personal way, know what it is to face a seemingly no-win situation that appears impossible to overcome?

I do. And that challenge taught me one of the most important and powerful lessons you and I can ever learn as believers about the gift of prayer.

It all began a year and a half after I was called to First Baptist Atlanta as the associate pastor. The senior pastor had resigned, and several members of the pulpit committee suggested that I fill his role. As I prayed about it, God showed me it was His will for me to be senior pastor of the church. I continued to serve—preaching every Sunday morning and evening—as the committee deliberated. First Baptist began to change and grow spiritually.

That's when the conflict arose. There were seven very affluent and influential members of the congregation who didn't like the fact that I sought the Lord's direction for every decision or the way I taught from God's Word. They began to spread false accusations about me. Sadly, many people believed their fabrications and joined in the effort to get rid of me.

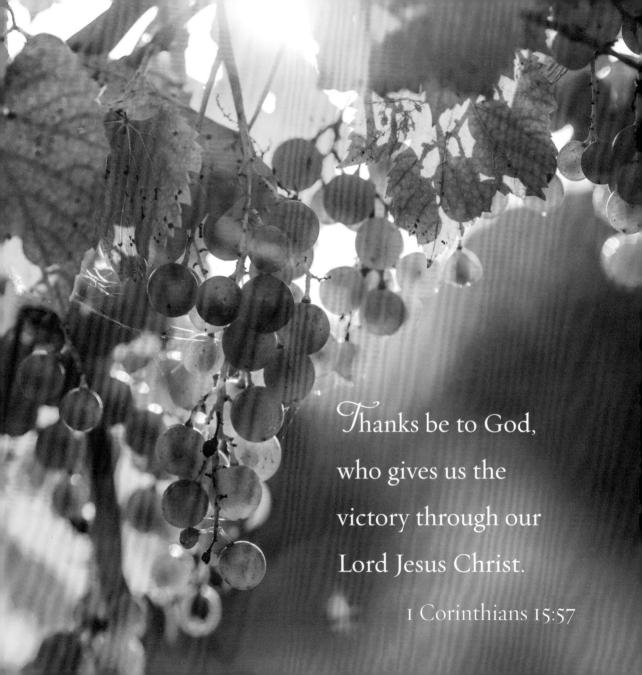

Thanks be to God,
who gives us the
victory through our
Lord Jesus Christ.

1 Corinthians 15:57

I remember how difficult and disheartening it was to walk out on Sunday morning and preach, knowing that so many church members bitterly despised everything I said and represented. I recall going to the prayer room often and even telling God that I didn't want to be their pastor. But during that time, the Father taught me that extremely important lesson I mentioned.

He said, "If you want to win this battle, you must fight it on your knees alone with Me." He made it very clear: "Do not argue or stand up for yourself. Remain faithful to Me. I will protect you."

Forty years later, I can say with great joy that the Lord has been absolutely faithful in fulfilling everything He taught and promised me. He fought for me, defended me, and triumphed in that impossible situation.

Is there a challenge you're facing? Are there people or circumstances aligned against you in your health, finances, career, relationships, or walk with the Lord? God will allow you to face some battles in your life. Some will be difficult and disheartening because other people will be involved. At other times, the war will be against your own limitations in order to stretch your faith. But the most important thing for you to remember whenever you face a battle is that there can be only one Commander in Chief, and if you want to be victorious, that role can be filled only by God. As Proverbs 21:31 states, "Victory belongs to the LORD." It belongs to Him; it is His possession. You don't have to take the lead or manipulate your circumstances. On the contrary, your combat strategy must begin and end with confidence that the Lord is in control of your situation and that He is actively resolving it for you when you obey Him.

This is why I always say, "Fight your battles on your knees, and you'll win every time." When you are tackling the conflicts before you in prayer, you are in the perfect posture to triumph. This is one of the most powerful, impactful gifts that prayer can provide you—you are embracing the victory God has already won for you.

How do you fight your battles on your knees? *First, you do so by setting aside time alone with the Father.* It is easy to be distracted when conflicts arise. You become so busy fretting about your troubles and running after solutions that you fail to turn to the One who can best help you (Psalm 103:19). Therefore, schedule time to focus solely on the Lord. Let nothing interrupt your communion with Him, because it is crucial to your success.

Second, listen quietly to the Father and expect Him to speak to you. Prayer

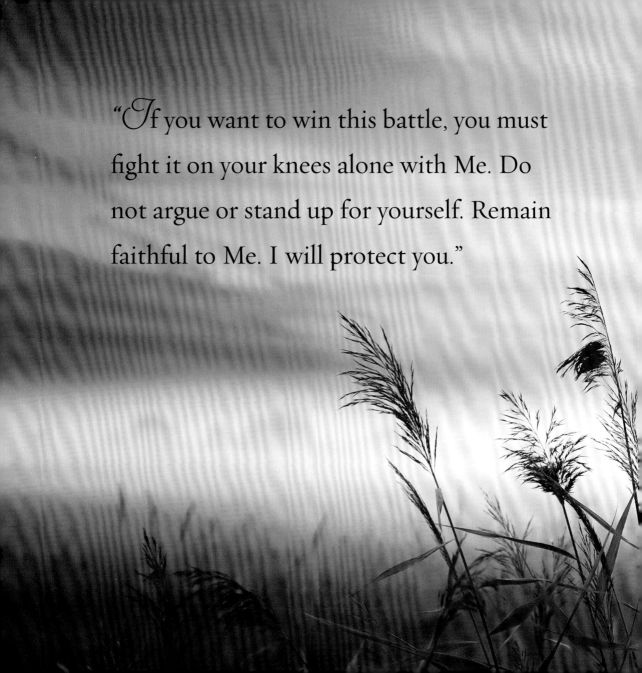

"If you want to win this battle, you must fight it on your knees alone with Me. Do not argue or stand up for yourself. Remain faithful to Me. I will protect you."

is not just telling the Lord how you feel—although that is part of it. Rather, He wants to reveal Himself to you and direct you in the way you should go. As Ecclesiastes 5:1–2 instructs, "Guard your steps as you go to the house of God and draw near to listen. . . . For God is in heaven and you are on the earth; therefore let your words be few." He has a better perspective on what is happening than you do, so pay attention to Him and obey His direction.

Third, as I've repeated often throughout this book, if the Lord reveals any sinfulness in your life, repent of it immediately. Remember, the Father's primary goal is to have an intimate relationship with you. When sin is present, it is evidence that you are hindering Him from having full access to your life. Therefore, agree with God about your iniquity and allow Him to teach you. He will show you how to change the way you operate for maximum intimacy with Him, effectiveness in your life, and influence with others.

Fourth, as I just mentioned, remember there can be only one Commander in Chief in this battle—and that's the Lord. God willingly employs His supernatural power in defending you, training you, and bringing out your full potential. However, you must be willing to acknowledge that He is in control and knows the path ahead better than you do. This is absolutely crucial as you continue to confront this difficulty, because in order to achieve the awesome victory He has envisioned, you must first surrender yourself to Him.

Fifth, see everything that happens to you as coming from God. Why would you do this? Because, as we've already discussed, if the Father allows a trial or challenge in your life, it is ultimately for your good and His glory (Romans 8:28). Knowing that He has permitted the troubles in your life for your benefit makes it easier to forgive those who hurt you and accept the seemingly inexplicable circumstances you must bear.

The truth is, you and I are always going to encounter struggles until we go home to heaven. However, God has promised, "No weapon that is formed against you will prosper; and every tongue that accuses you in judgment you will condemn. This is the heritage of the servants of the LORD, and their vindication is from Me" (Isaiah 54:17). And He has given you the gift of prayer as your defense against whatever assails you.

When you fight your battles on your knees and faithfully obey Him, you invite God to be your Redeemer, Defender, General, and Protector. That's the most wonderful, eternal path to triumph every single time. So as I have said repeatedly throughout this book—*pray*!

In order to achieve the awesome victory God has envisioned, you must first surrender yourself to Him.

It is an awesome gift. A victory-ensuring gift. And rejoice that you are overwhelmingly more than a conqueror through Christ who loves you (Romans 8:37; 1 Corinthians 15:57).

Father, how grateful I am for Your protection, guidance, and strength. Thank You for being my Commander in Chief through the gift of prayer! Truly, there is no Defender, Warrior, or King like You—in heaven or on earth. Regardless of the enemies or challenges on my path, You overcome them easily. No matter the conflicts and trials we face, You are always triumphant.

Father, help me not to become angry or defensive, but always turn to You when conflicts arise. Thank You for always being available to me and leading me to victory regardless of the battle. Help me to wait on Your perfect timing, trust You every step of the way, and be willing to obey all You ask.

In Jesus' holy, wise, and powerful name I pray. Amen.

Taking Hold
of the GIFT

As we inquire of God, anticipate His speaking, respond to what we hear, are alert to His confirmations, and simply ask Him to speak clearly, we set the stage for the greatest adventure known to man—hearing almighty God deliver His message to us.

What greater privilege, what greater responsibility could we desire?

11

FINDING YOUR FUTURE AT THE THRONE

*D*o you look forward to the future with hope and anticipation? Or do you face it with dread? Does the thought of the days ahead fill you with joy at the opportunities that lay before you? Or does it stir up anxiety and trepidation because of the trials you may encounter?

I can say personally I cannot help but be encouraged because I believe that the best is still to come. Why do I have such a steadfast conviction? Because over the years, God has taught me that I can always have absolute confidence in Him. You see, back in the 1970s, I had no idea about all the awesome things the Father was going to do. The future was unknown to me and seemed to hold many challenges. All I knew was that the Lord had promised that if I would engage with Him through the awesome gift of prayer and listen to and obey Him in faith, He would show me what to do.

As Proverbs 3:5–6 teaches, "Trust in the LORD with all your heart and do not lean on your own understanding. In all your ways acknowledge Him, and He will make your paths straight."

With this in mind, I remember praying with my coworkers that we could take the message of salvation outside the walls of the church.

Soon thereafter, God provided the opportunity for First Baptist Church to broadcast a simple thirty-minute program called *The Chapel Hour* on WXIA-TV 11 and WANX 46. Then, TBS on Channel 17 gave us a time slot to preach the gospel. Afterward, the Christian Broadcasting Network (CBN) called and asked to use some of our sermon tapes. We just kept trusting God, and doors kept opening.

Then one day in 1977, I was sitting in my study and thinking, *We need to give this program a name.* I looked over to my left, and there was a Living Bible on my desk. It was titled *In Touch.* I thought, *That's the name. God, that's what I want to do—I want to get as many people as possible in touch with Jesus Christ and His way of life.* Why? Because I knew that this is life at its very best—the life centered on Jesus Christ and walking with Him in obedience.

If there is anything that these years of preaching the gospel have taught me, it's that apart from salvation and the indwelling presence of the Holy Spirit, prayer is the greatest gift we have ever been given. That is because it gives us access to the One who knows all things and can do all things—and He "is able to do far more abundantly beyond all that we ask or think, according to the power that works within us" (Ephesians 3:20).

To Him who is able to do far more abundantly beyond all that we ask or think, according to the power that works within us, to Him be the glory in the church and in Christ Jesus to all generations forever and ever. Amen.

Ephesians 3:20–21

Remember, Hebrews 4:16 admonishes, "Let us draw near with confidence to the throne of grace, so that we may receive mercy and find grace to help in time of need." Have you ever truly considered the seat of power you have been invited to approach? This is the chair of ultimate authority—the everlasting throne of the only living God, supreme Sovereign of all creation.

Likewise, Hebrews 7:25 tells you Jesus "always lives to make intercession" for you. And friend, your Savior does not pray woeful or unsure prayers. He does not intercede as we often do—hesitantly and bound by limitations. No, Jesus prays with authority, wisdom, and unmeasurable ability!

He is the Great I Am, all-powerful and all-wise, who called the heavens and the earth into existence. Psalm 33:9 tells us, "When he spoke, the world began! It appeared at his command" (NLT). When He speaks out for you, *everything moves*. When He commands, *all must obey*. And that, friend, is the voice that intercedes *for you*. He is orchestrating and directing the circumstances of your life in unimaginable ways to draw you closer to Him and develop you for all those wonderful purposes He created you to fulfill.

Do you see why prayer is such a precious and priceless gift? It is the way you tap into that universe-moving power source and His eternal wisdom. It is the manner by which you can know the One who energizes and empowers you, shapes your future, gives you peace, transforms you and those around you, and ensures the ultimate victory.

Are you in touch with the Savior? Are you listening to God in order to walk with Him in the extraordinary life He has for you? He wants you to hear Him. In fact, Deuteronomy 4:29–31 promises, "You will seek the LORD your God, and you will find Him if you search for Him with all your heart and all your soul. When you are in distress . . . return to the LORD your God and listen to His voice. For the LORD your God is a compassionate God; He will not fail you."

Friend, do not ignore the mighty One who calls out to you. Listen to Him! Seek the Father *reflectively*. Meditate on His Word and think about its principles. Scripture contains God's thoughts and solutions for everything you will ever encounter. Therefore, read the Bible daily and seek His instruction.

Pray to God *actively*. Go to Him with a listening ear, asking the Holy Spirit to show you what He wants you to learn, and rely on His help to apply it to your life. He will remind you of all the Father is teaching you and show you how to proceed.

Third, obey the Lord *submissively*. Remember the admonition of Ecclesiastes 5:2: "Do not be hasty in word or impulsive in thought to bring up a matter in the presence of God. For God is in heaven and you are on the earth; therefore let your words be few." He knows how to lead you in the best manner possible. Therefore, be willing to obey whatever He commands.

Fourth, listen to the Father *expectantly*. God promises to speak to you, and He will. It may be through His Word, through others, or through your circumstances, but you can be certain He will guide you in what you should do.

Fifth, pray to the Lord *patiently*. There will be times when God teaches you His ways and His will at a pace slower than you expect or desire. Continue seeking His face and obeying regardless of how long it takes, assured that He works on behalf of those who wait for Him (Isaiah 64:4). Pray and keep praying, because what He can achieve through you will absolutely astonish you if you will stay the course and trust Him.

Are you willing? Will you look forward to the future with joy and anticipation by engaging in the gift of prayer? I hope you will, because I have no doubt that it will be beyond your greatest expectations if

Life at its very best is the life centered on Jesus Christ and walking with Him in obedience.

Prayer is such a priceless gift
because it is the way you tap
into the universe-moving power
source and His eternal wisdom.

you will carefully seek God reflectively, actively, submissively, expectantly, and patiently.

I have certainly seen that to be true. From those days in the 1970s when my coworkers and I prayed for God to take the message of salvation outside the walls of First Baptist Atlanta, He has astounded us. He has allowed the ministry to grow outside the boundaries of Atlanta, out of Georgia, out of the United States, out of North America, and on into every country on the planet—exceedingly far and abundantly farther than we ever hoped or imagined.

Take hold of this amazing gift of prayer and find your future at the throne of grace. Stay in touch with your wonderful Savior. Heed His call so you can walk with Him. He will heal your wounds, break through the barriers you encounter, overcome the obstacles you face, and attain victory over any challenges that assail you.

Listen to the voice of the One who moves the heavens and the earth on your behalf for the purpose of giving you an awesome, eternal hope. Because that is the path to life at its very best, and He will surely surprise you with all the blessings He's planned for you.

My beloved Father, who is in heaven, hallowed—holy and exalted—is Your name. Thank You for this wonderful gift of prayer You have given me and for Your wonderful plan for my life. Father, may Your kingdom come—may Your gospel be preached throughout the earth and may people acknowledge that You are the King of kings and the Lord of lords. May every knee bow, and may every tongue confess that Jesus is Lord. May Your will be done—on earth as it is in heaven—especially in and through my life. Lord, I want to find my future at Your throne. I know that You speak and make a way for me. You command, and closed doors are opened in a manner no one can shut. Help me to listen to You reflectively, actively, submissively, expectantly, and patiently. When I cannot hear Your voice, give me the endurance to keep seeking You and Your will.

Father, thank You for all You do on my behalf. I thank You for my daily bread and that You take care of all my needs—even the ones that appear unmet at the moment. Thank You for pardoning my sins and helping me forgive those who hurt me. Thank You for helping me fight and escape temptation so I can live a holy life that honors You. Thank You for delivering me from evil and from the bondage to sin.

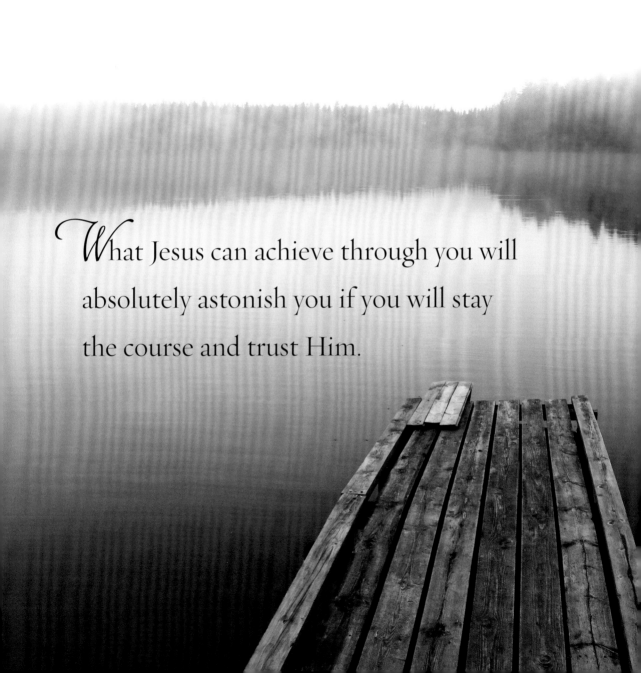

What Jesus can achieve through you will
absolutely astonish you if you will stay
the course and trust Him.

For Yours is the kingdom and the power and the glory forever, Lord Jesus. You are my Savior, my Authority, and the great Giver of this wonderful gift of prayer. I look forward to the future with joy, expectation, and anticipation, knowing that You lead me perfectly and are worthy of all my respect, worship, obedience, and adoration.

Thank You for leading me to life at its best. To You be all honor and praise forever.

In Jesus' awesome, holy, and glorious name I pray. Amen.

*T*ake hold of this amazing gift of prayer and find your future at the throne of grace.

ABOUT THE AUTHOR

*D*r. Charles Stanley is the senior pastor of the First Baptist Church of Atlanta, Georgia, where he has served for fifty years. He is a *New York Times* bestselling author who has written more than sixty books, including the top devotional *Every Day in His Presence*. Dr. Stanley is the founder of In Touch Ministries. The *In Touch with Dr. Charles Stanley* program is transmitted throughout the world on more than 1,200 radio outlets, 130 television stations/networks, and in language projects in more than 50 languages. The award-winning *In Touch* devotional magazine is printed in four languages, with more than 12 million copies each year. Dr. Stanley's goal is best represented by Acts 20:24: "Life is worth nothing unless I use it for doing the work assigned me by the Lord Jesus—the work of telling others the Good News about God's mighty kindness and love" (TLB). This is because, as he says, "It is the Word of God and the work of God that changes people's lives."